- ☐ **Make coffee.**
- ☐ **GET SHIT DONE.**
- ☐ **Repeat.**

This journal belongs to:

_____

Elys Journals

www.ingramcontent.com/pod-product-compliance
Lightning Source LLC
Chambersburg PA
CBHW070437180526
45158CB00019B/1527